W9-AOK-256

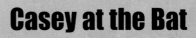

Casey at the Bat

ERNEST L. THAYER

# CASEY AT THE BAT

WITH ILLUSTRATIONS BY
JOE MORSE

KCP POETRY
AN IMPRINT OF KIDS CAN PRESS

THE OUTLOOK WASN'T BRILLIANT
FOR THE MUDVILLE NINE THAT DAY:
THE SCORE STOOD FOUR TO TWO,
WITH BUT ONE INNING MORE TO PLAY,

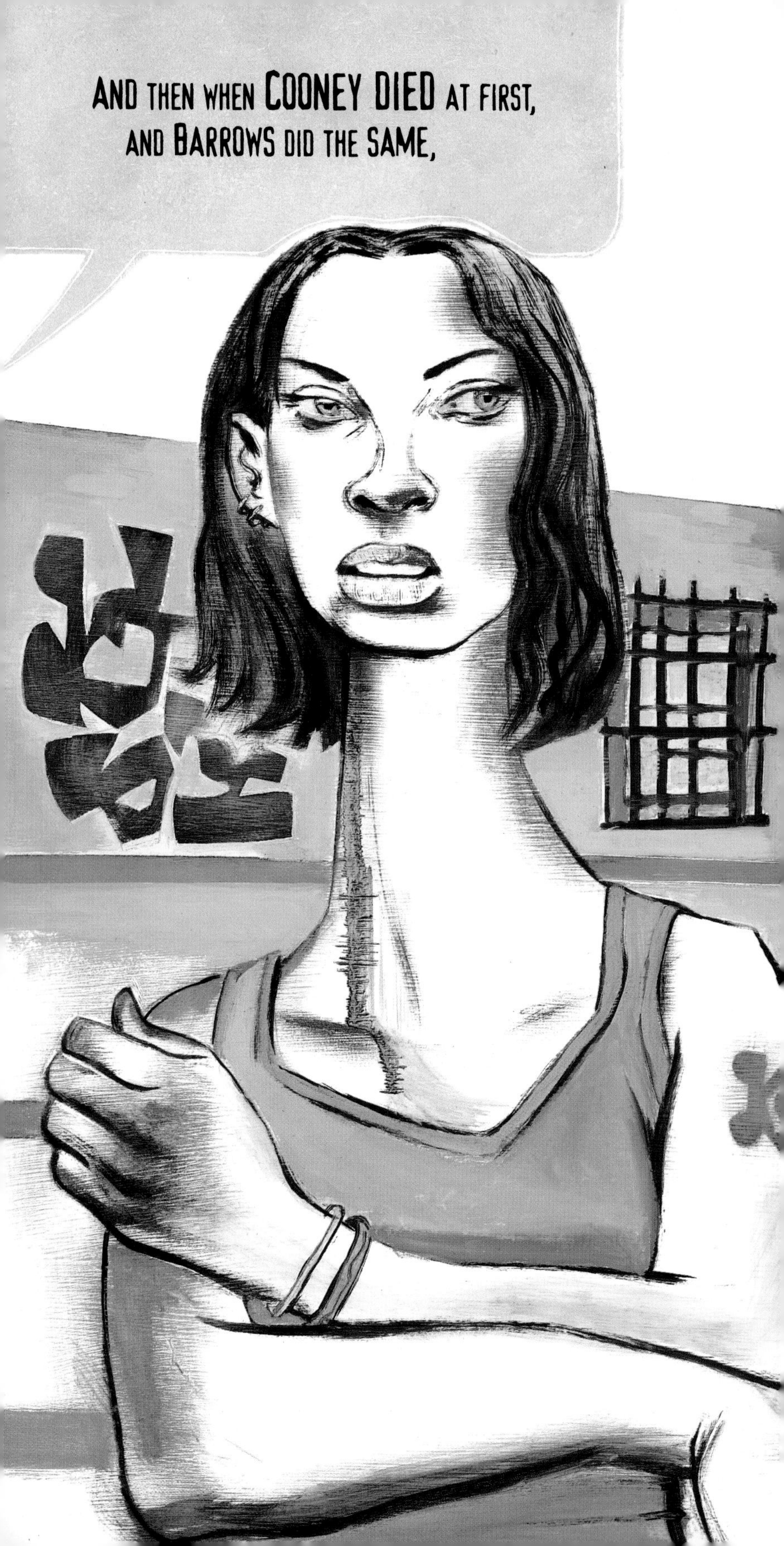
AND THEN WHEN COONEY DIED AT FIRST, AND BARROWS DID THE SAME,

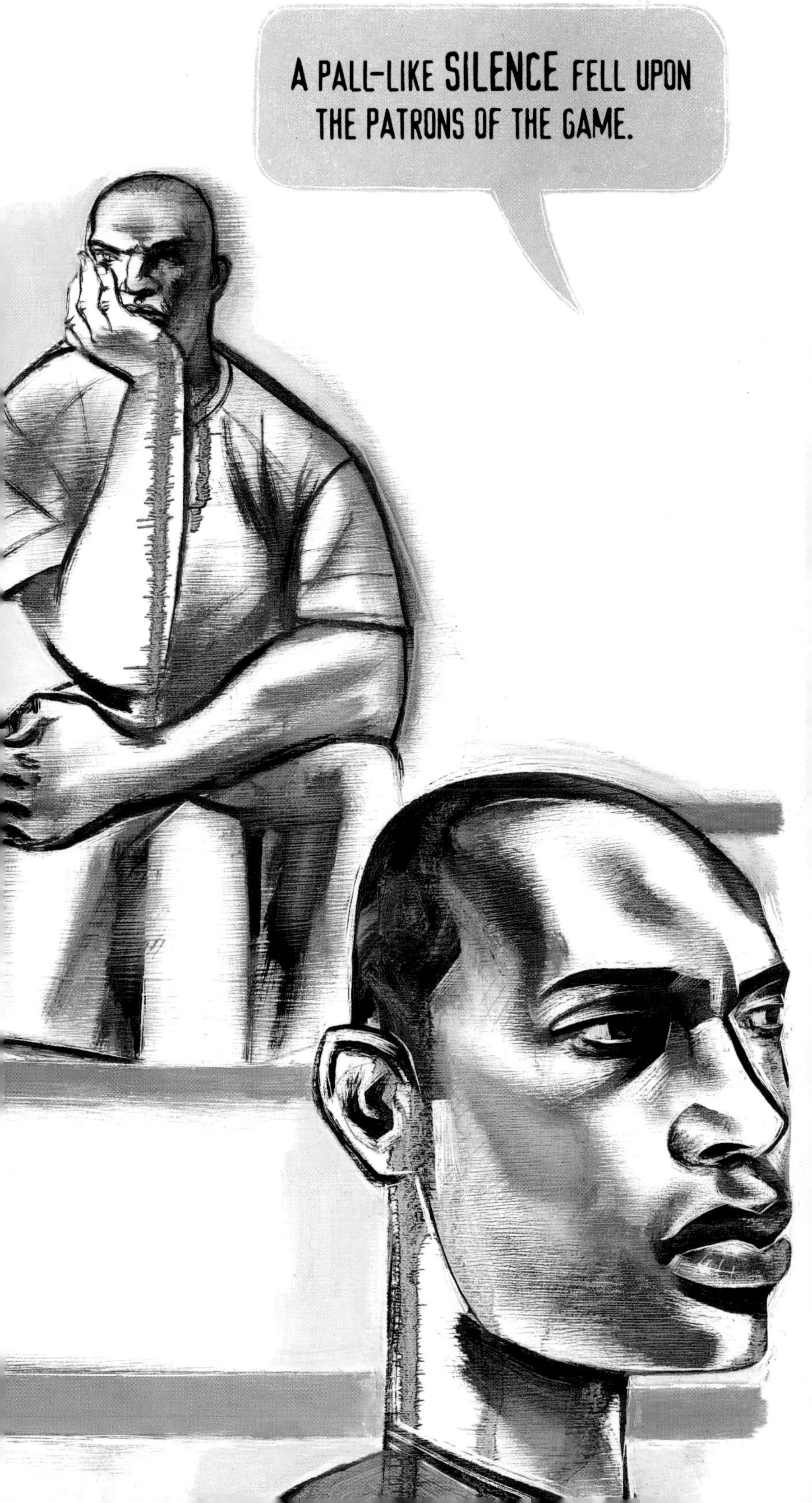
A PALL-LIKE SILENCE FELL UPON THE PATRONS OF THE GAME.

A STRAGGLING FEW GOT UP TO GO IN DEEP DESPAIR. THE REST CLUNG TO THAT HOPE WHICH SPRINGS ETERNAL IN THE HUMAN BREAST;

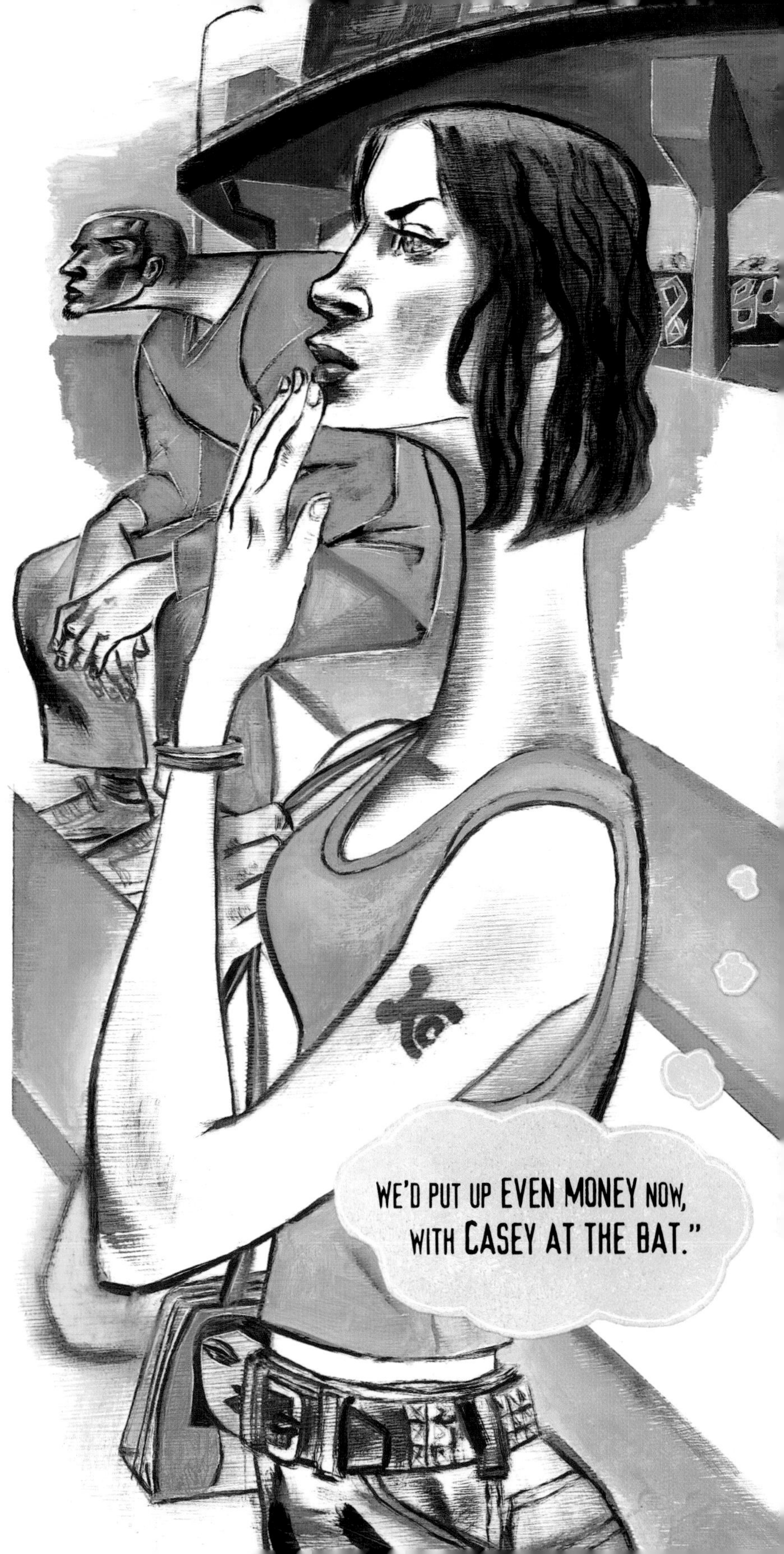
WE'D PUT UP EVEN MONEY NOW, WITH CASEY AT THE BAT."

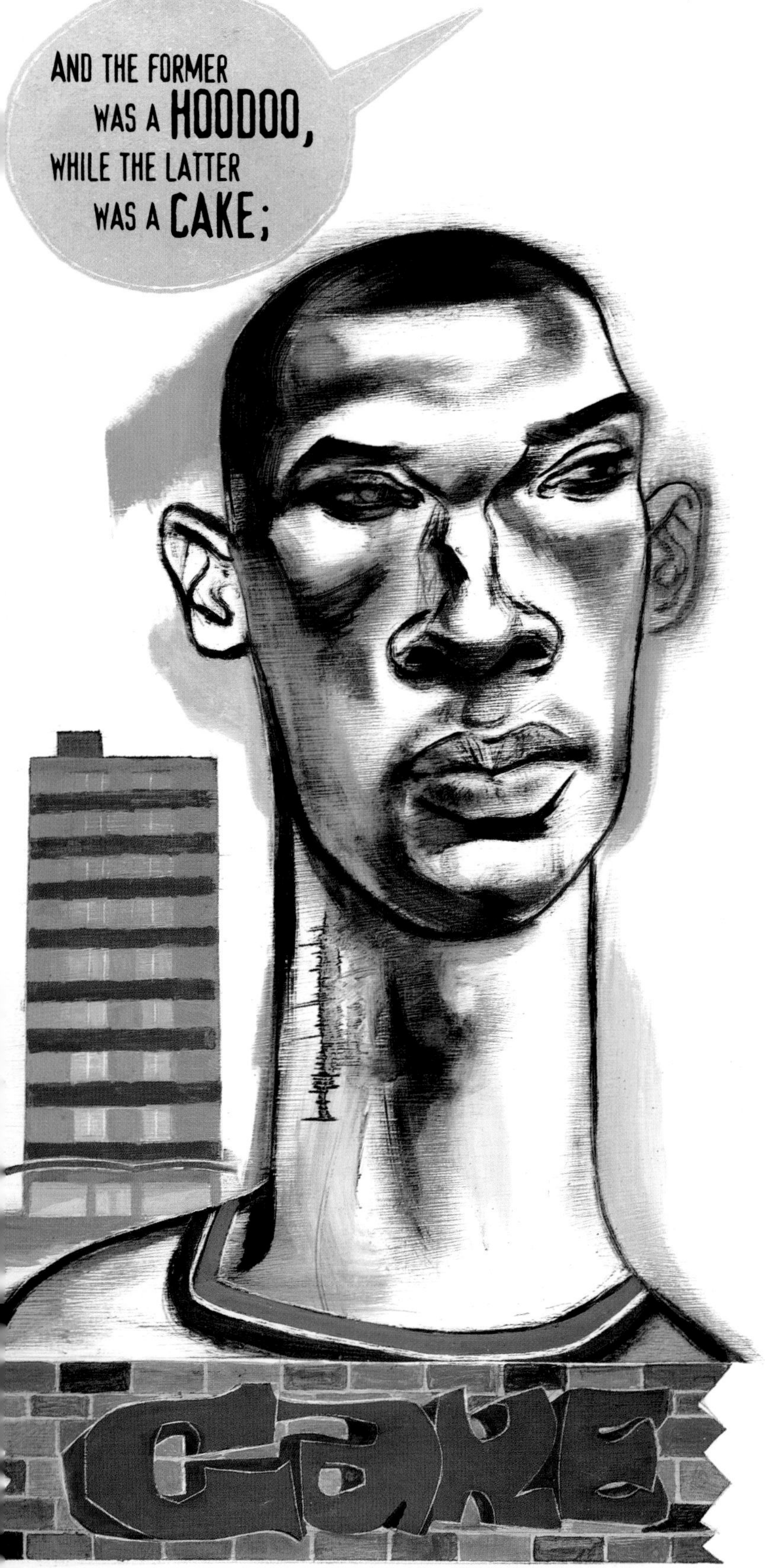
AND THE FORMER WAS A HOODOO, WHILE THE LATTER WAS A CAKE;
CAKE

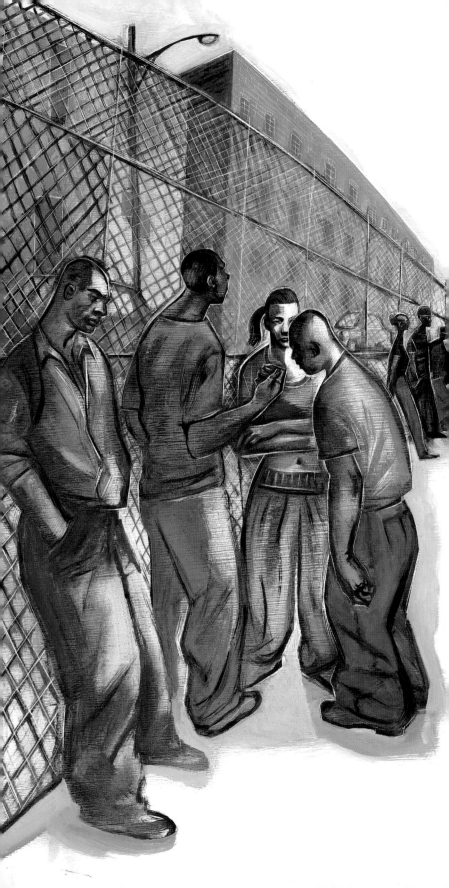

UPON THAT STRICKEN MULTITUDE
GRIM MELANCHOLY SAT,
R THERE SEEMED BUT LITTLE CHANCE
OF CASEY GETTING TO THE BAT.

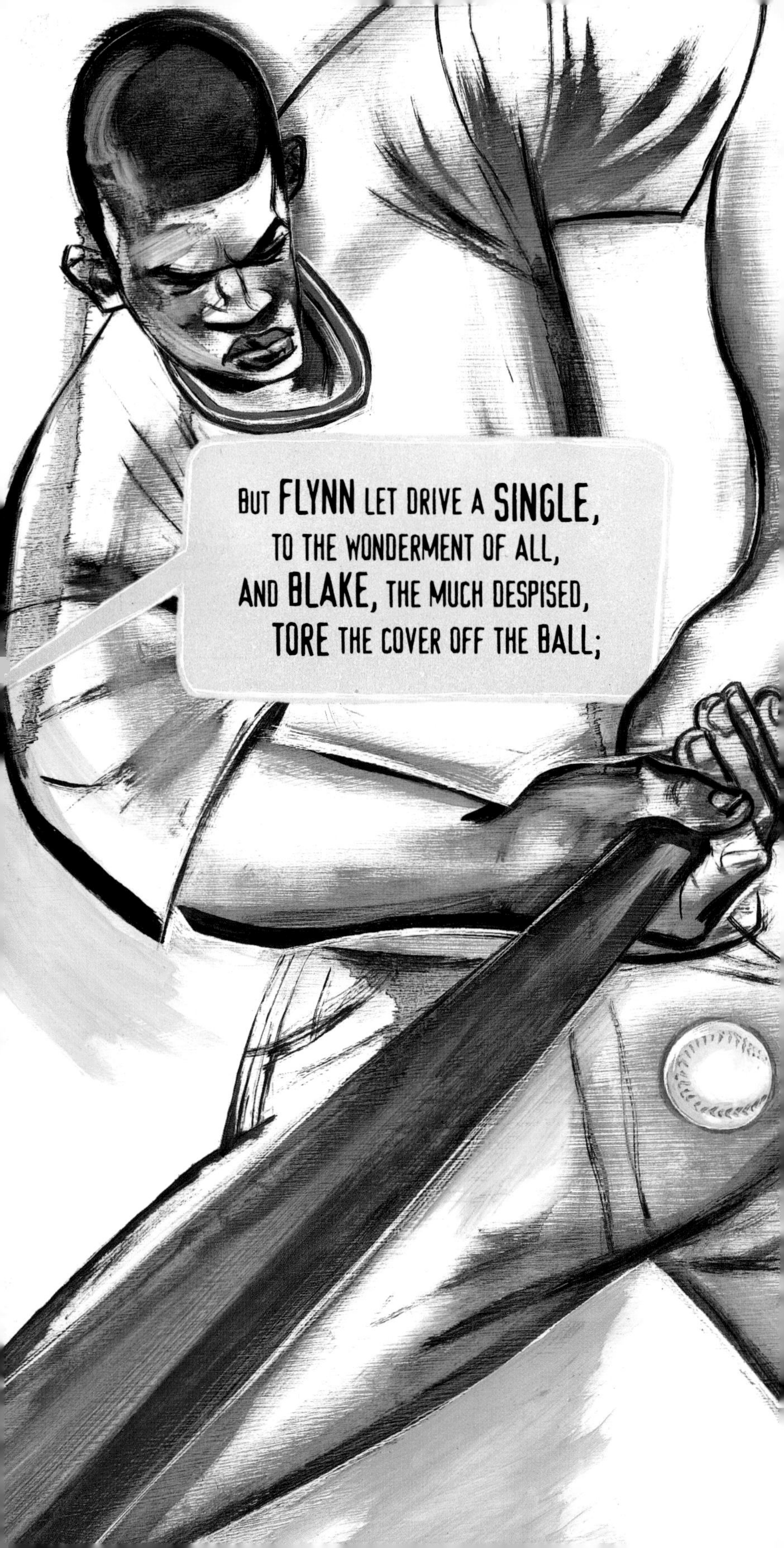
BUT FLYNN LET DRIVE A SINGLE,
TO THE WONDERMENT OF ALL,
AND BLAKE, THE MUCH DESPISED,
TORE THE COVER OFF THE BALL;

2nd
AND WHEN THE DUST HAD LIFTED,
AND MEN SAW WHAT HAD OCCURRED,
THERE WAS JIMMY SAFE AT SECOND
AND FLYNN A-HUGGING
THIRD.
3rd

THEN FROM **FIVE THOUSAND** THROATS AND MORE THERE ROSE A LUSTY **YELL**; IT **RUMBLED** THROUGH THE VALLEY, IT **RATTLED** IN THE DELL; IT **POUNDED** ON THE MOUNTAIN AND RECOILED UPON THE FLAT,

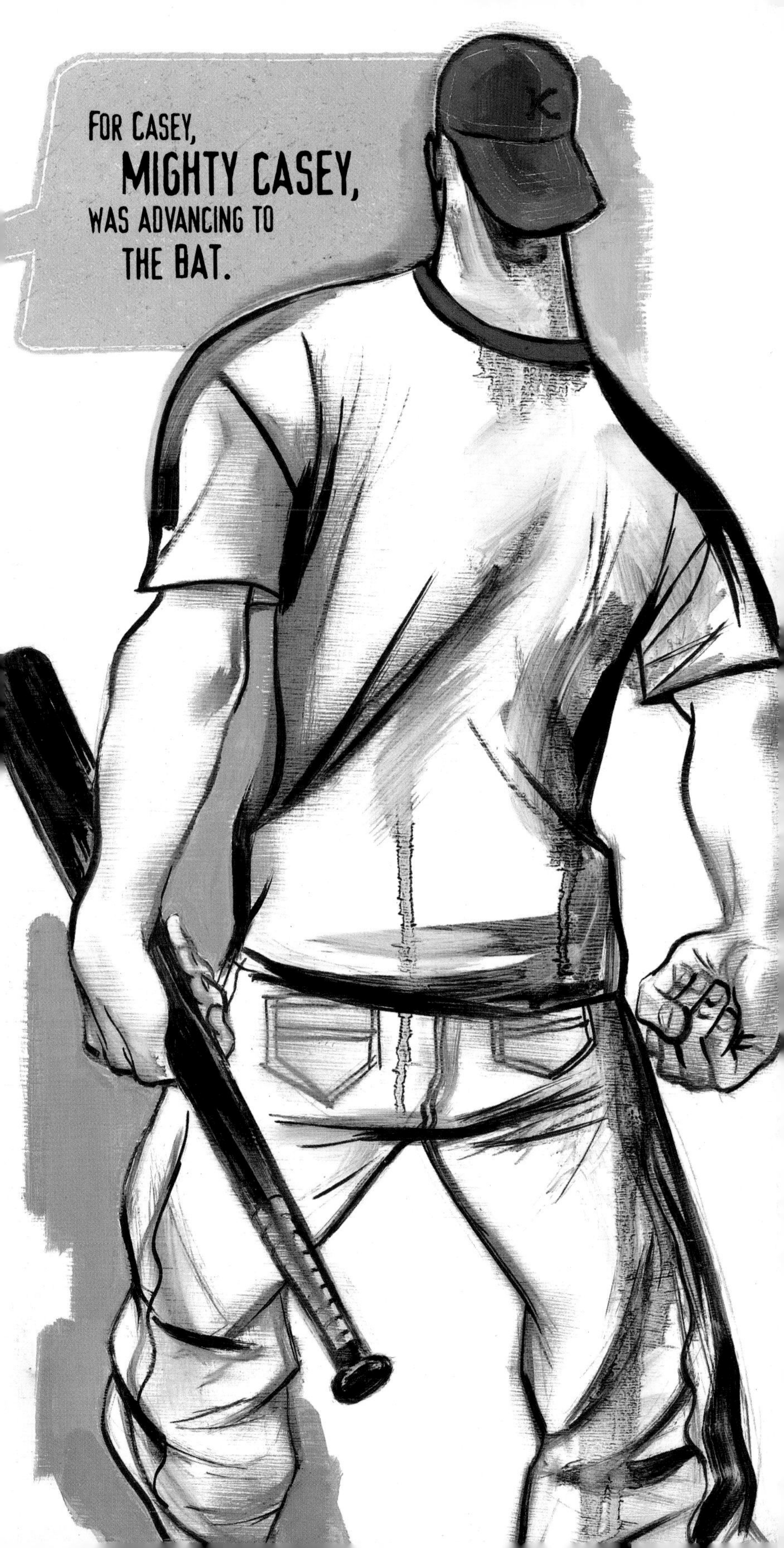
FOR CASEY,
MIGHTY CASEY,
WAS ADVANCING TO
THE BAT.

There was EASE in Casey's manner
as he stepped into his place;
There was PRIDE in Casey's bearing
and a SMILE lit Casey's face.

AND WHEN, RESPONDING TO THE **CHEERS**,
HE LIGHTLY DOFFED HIS HAT,
NO STRANGER IN THE **CROWD** COULD DOUBT
'TWAS **CASEY** AT THE BAT.

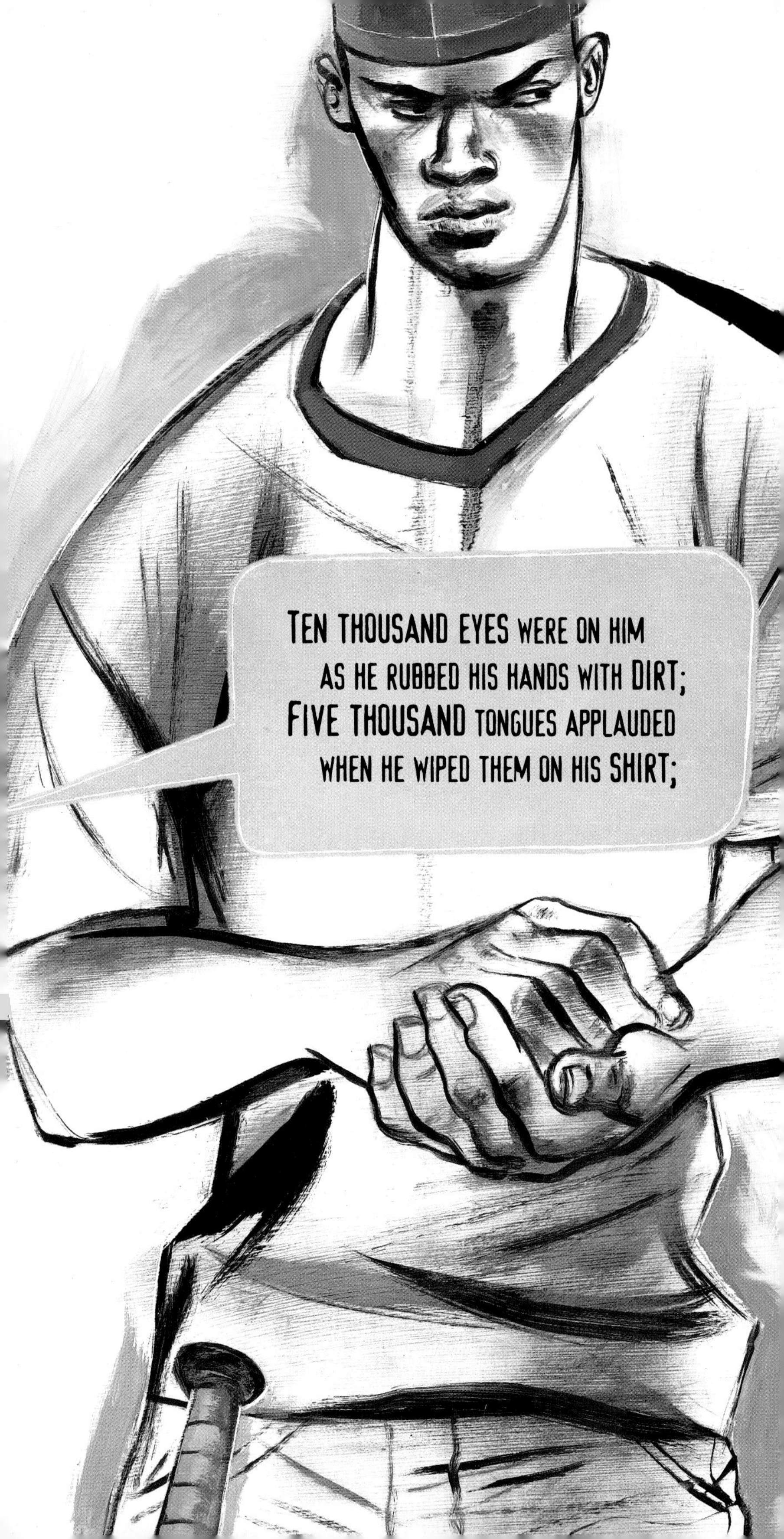
TEN THOUSAND EYES WERE ON HIM AS HE RUBBED HIS HANDS WITH DIRT; FIVE THOUSAND TONGUES APPLAUDED WHEN HE WIPED THEM ON HIS SHIRT;

THEN WHILE THE WRITHING PITCHER
GROUND THE BALL INTO HIS HIP,
**DEFIANCE** FLASHED
IN CASEY'S EYE,
A SNEER CURLED CASEY'S LIP.

AND NOW THE LEATHER-COVERED SPHERE CAME **HURTLING** THROUGH THE AIR,

AND **CASEY** STOOD A-WATCHING IT IN HAUGHTY GRANDEUR THERE

"**THAT AIN'T MY STYLE,**" SAID CASEY.

CLOSE BY THE STURDY BATSMAN THE BALL **UNHEEDED** SPED —

FROM THE BENCHES, BLACK WITH PEOPLE,
THERE WENT UP A MUFFLED ROAR,
LIKE THE BEATING OF THE STORM-WAVES
ON A STERN AND DISTANT SHORE;
"KILL HIM! KILL THE UMPIRE!"
SHOUTED SOMEONE ON THE STAND;
AND IT'S LIKELY THEY'D HAVE KILLED HIM
HAD NOT CASEY RAISED HIS HAND.

WITH A SMILE OF CHRISTIAN CHARITY
  GREAT **CASEY'S** VISAGE SHONE;
HE STILLED THE RISING TUMULT;
  HE BADE THE GAME GO ON;
HE SIGNALED TO THE PITCHER,
  AND ONCE MORE THE DUN SPHERE FLEW;
BUT CASEY STILL IGNORED IT,

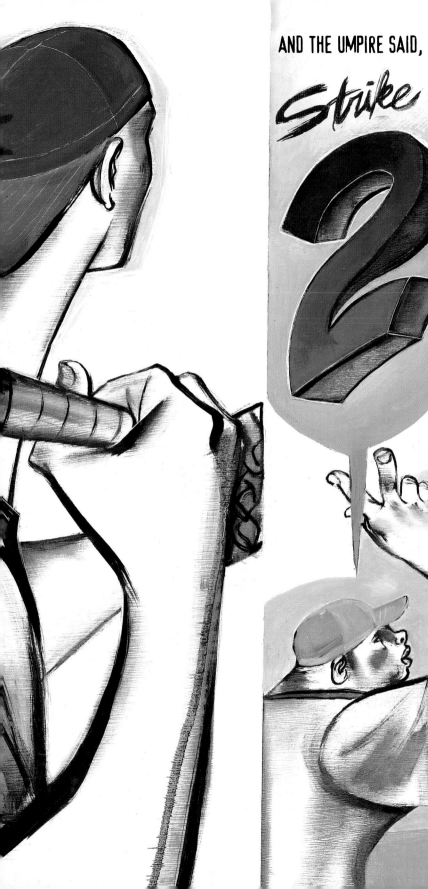

"FRAUD!" CRIED THE
MADDENED THOUSANDS,
AND ECHO ANSWERED "FRAUD!"
BUT ONE SCORNFUL LOOK FROM CASEY
AND THE AUDIENCE WAS AWED.

THEY SAW HIS FACE GROW **STERN** AND COLD,
THEY SAW HIS **MUSCLES** STRAIN,
AND THEY KNEW THAT CASEY WOULDN'T LET
THAT BALL **GO BY AGAIN.**

THE SNEER HAS FLED FROM CASEY'S LIP,
HIS TEETH ARE CLENCHED IN HATE;
HE POUNDS WITH CRUEL VIOLENCE
HIS BAT UPON THE PLATE.

AND NOW THE PITCHER HOLDS THE BALL, AND NOW HE LETS IT GO,

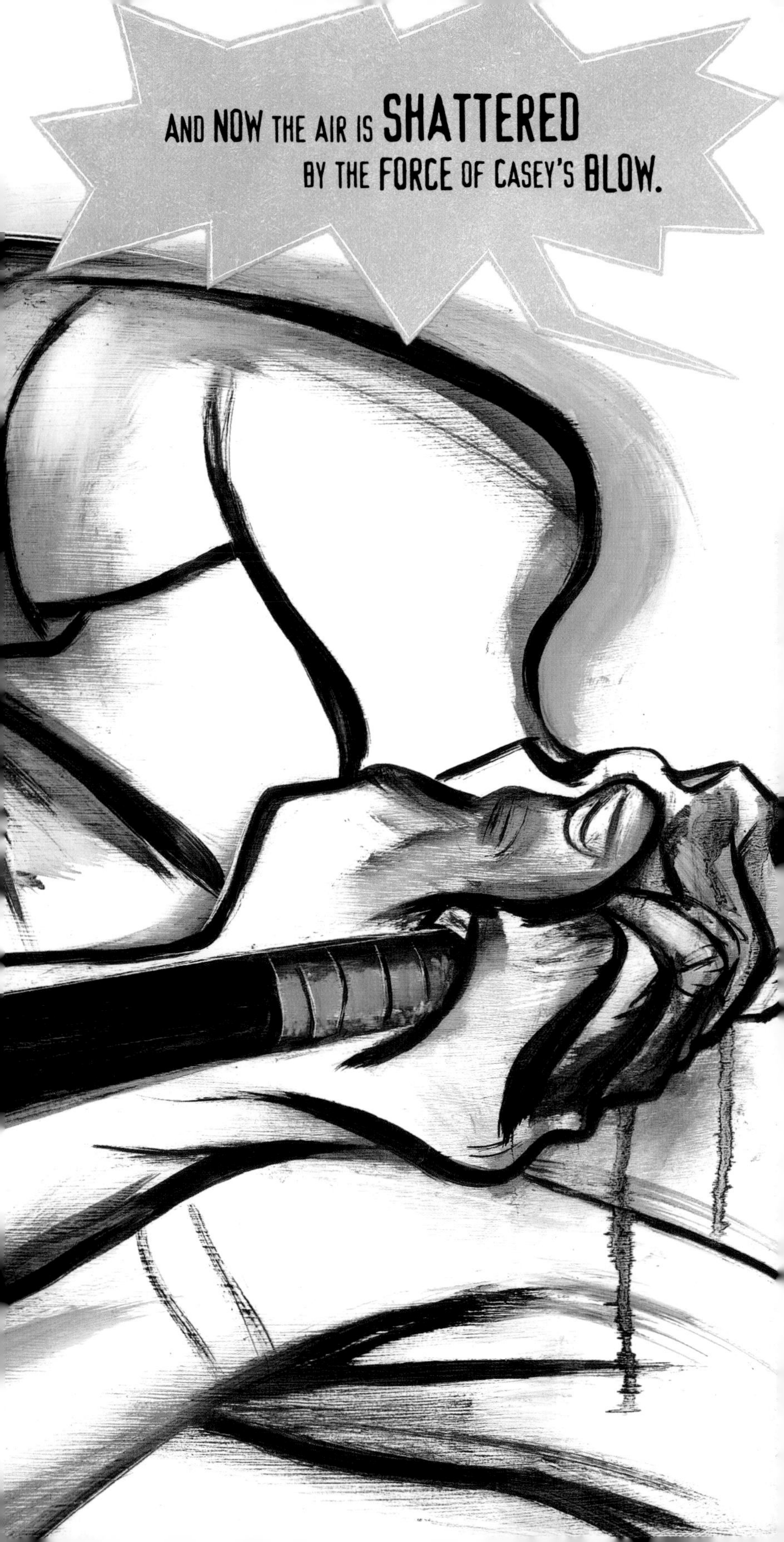
AND NOW THE AIR IS SHATTERED
BY THE FORCE OF CASEY'S BLOW.

OH, SOMEWHERE IN THIS FAVORED LAND
    THE SUN IS SHINING BRIGHT;
THE BAND IS PLAYING SOMEWHERE,
    AND SOMEWHERE HEARTS ARE LIGHT,
AND SOMEWHERE MEN ARE LAUGHING,
    AND LITTLE CHILDREN SHOUT;

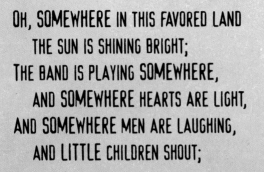

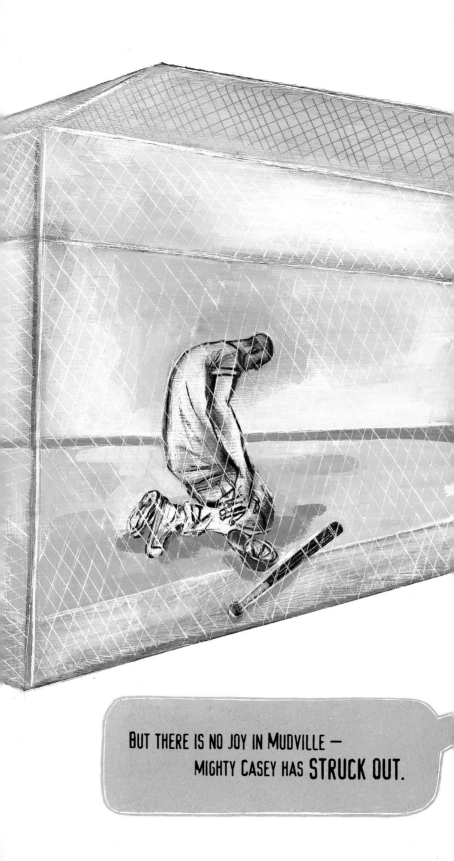

But there is no joy in Mudville —
Mighty Casey has **STRUCK OUT.**

# Ernest L. Thayer

American writer and poet Ernest Lawrence Thayer (1863–1940) is perhaps best known today as the author of "Casey at the Bat." After graduating from Harvard in 1885, where he was the editor of the *Harvard Lampoon*, Thayer began working as a humor columnist for the *San Francisco Examiner*. "Casey at the Bat: A Ballad of the Republic, Sung in the Year 1888" appeared in the June 3, 1888, issue under Thayer's byline, "Phin." But it took a recitation of the poem later that year by actor De Wolf Hopper, at a show for the New York Giants and the Chicago White Stockings, for it to gain notoriety. Hopper didn't discover who wrote the ballad until Thayer attended one of his by-then legendary performances of "Casey" about five years later and granted the actor rights to recite the poem without paying any royalties. It was well into the 1900s, however, before Thayer was widely accepted as the true author. Thayer's reluctance to assert his claim to "Casey" seems to have something to do with the fact that he considered it one of his mediocre works, remarking, "Its persistent vogue is simply unaccountable, and it would be hard to say, all things considered, if it has given me more pleasure than annoyance."

Despite its creator's modest opinion, "Casey" remains one of the most treasured poems in the English language. It is a poem that is as much a part of baseball as hot dogs, the national anthem and the seventh-inning stretch. Yet its appeal is not limited to enthusiasts of the sport or of poetry. "Casey" has been recited in theatres, ballparks and classrooms, and has inspired parodies, sequels, books, films, operas, paintings, cartoons and television shows. Thayer's poem is a part of the very fabric of American culture, a status that was confirmed in 1996 when the United States Postal Service issued a Casey stamp as part of a series saluting American folk heroes. Although "the outlook wasn't brilliant for the Mudville nine that day," the future of Thayer's fictional slugger proved to be very bright indeed; Mighty Casey struck out that fateful day in Mudville, but he has been immortalized in verse, bringing joy to generations of fans.

# Joe Morse

Joe Morse's vision of "Casey at the Bat" marks a bold departure from the many nostalgically illustrated editions of the poem. Reinventing this American classic for a new generation, Morse portrays the cool, swaggering Casey (a.k.a. KC) and his Mudville 9 as a group of multiracial inner-city kids playing ball in an urban jungle of concrete buildings, chain-link fences and graffiti-covered walls. It is a particularly relevant approach in an era where kids dream of escaping their present-day realities by following in the footsteps of the sports figures they idolize.

Although Morse has put a contemporary spin on "Casey," his powerful depiction of the intensity, emotion and drama of the verse and of baseball itself stays true to the poem's spirit. Morse's images paint a compelling portrait of human nature, particularly the psychology of the hero and the crowd. Indeed, this interpretation of "Casey" transforms Thayer's caricatures into flesh-and-blood people with real hopes and dreams — and real vulnerability. Here, the muscular, towering figure of Mighty Casey is much more than an arrogant showman. He is someone who is ultimately confined by the batting cage and the concrete boxes of his surroundings, deserted by even his most ardent fans. Morse explores the idea of the hero in the context of modern culture, where the line between celebrity and heroism is sadly blurred. With Morse's singular vision and striking images, this hard-hitting edition of "Casey" is clearly a grand slam.

Joe Morse paints outside year round in headphones, a baseball cap and, due to the toxicity of his materials, a gas mask. His art is exhibited in numerous private and public collections in North America and has won many international honors, such as awards from the New York Society of Illustrators, *Communication Arts* and *American Illustration*. His impressive list of commercial clients includes Nike, *The New Yorker, Rolling Stone* and Universal Pictures. Director of the Degree Program in Illustration at Sheridan Institute, Morse lives in Toronto, Ontario, with his wife, artist Lorraine Tuson, and their two children.

To Lorraine, for making each of these pictures live,
and to my mother, Andrea, who has inspired me
with her love of all that life has to bring — J.M.

⌗

The illustrations for this book were
rendered in oil and acrylic on paper.

The text was set in
DEVICE and **Impact**

⌗

KCP Poetry is an imprint of Kids Can Press

Illustrations © 2006 Joe Morse

Kids Can Press acknowledges the financial support of the Government of
Ontario, through the Ontario Media Development Corporation's Ontario Book
Initiative; the Ontario Arts Council; the Canada Council for the Arts; and the
Government of Canada, through the BPIDP, for our publishing activity.

| Published in Canada by | Published in the U.S. by |
| --- | --- |
| Kids Can Press Ltd. | Kids Can Press Ltd. |
| 29 Birch Avenue | 2250 Military Road |
| Toronto, ON  M4V 1E2 | Tonawanda, NY  14150 |

www.kidscanpress.com

Edited by Tara Walker
Designed by Karen Powers
Printed and bound in China

This book is smyth sewn casebound.

CM 06  0 9 8 7 6 5 4 3 2 1

Library and Archives Canada Cataloguing in Publication

Thayer, Ernest Lawrence, 1863–1940
Casey at the bat / written by Ernest L. Thayer ; with illustrations by Joe Morse.

(Visions in poetry)

ISBN-13: 978-1-55337-827-3 (bound)     ISBN-10: 1-55337-827-X (bound)

1. Baseball — Poetry. I. Morse, Joe, 1960–  II. Title.  III. Series.

PS3014.T3C38 2006        811'.52        C2005-904232-X

Kids Can Press is a /orus™ Entertainment company